WINGSPAN

422 N. 4th Avenue
Tucson, Az. 85705 (602) 624-1779

Wingspan
300 E. Sixth Street
Tucson, Arizona 85705

for phoenix —
may you find or
create your dream
of wimin's community!
zana
jan. 1987

herb womon

poems and art

by

zana

some of these poems and drawings first appeared in
the following publications (some under the names
marilynn neel and marilynn woodsea):

    womanspirit
    off our backs
    focus, a journal for lesbians
    earthcircles
    the poet
    natural lighting
    WEB (wimmin of the earth bonding)
    common lives/lesbian lives
    northwoods journal
    day tonight/night today
    wayside quarterly
    labyris
    women's press
    telewoman
    rough road/new times
    listen to the valley
    changing images

printed by kate hitt,   bayside, california

for

pegasis, my love

carol, my sister

and may this book especially
be a gift for the many wimin who
have helped sustain me, body and soul,
in the rainbow light of womon-vision....

<u>contents</u>

we make
our own holidays

<u>gypsies</u>

"we'll share like gypsies," daddy said
swigging soda, passing it back to me
as he drove. he decided
we'd try to glimpse the fireworks from a hill
to avoid cotton bowl crowds.
carol dripped green snow-cone on my pink pants
elaine's little shoes flailed; she cried.
i hated mom's incomprehensible
sky-soft sunday smile.

    one hand on the wheel, loraine sings a song
    we play together on guitars.
    her son shares corn chips and kefir
    with julie in the back seat.
    this week's town trip: co-op, library,
    julie checking out the flea market,
    children's day in the park for zoe.
    the old toyota grunts through gears
    and we're off again for home, the highway a canvas
    for the brilliant colors of dream-making.
    in a quiet moment, i feel my smile soft as sun.
    mom, i wish you could be here.

we make our own holidays now
we, remembering arch of candles
we, remembering our child-images
looming out red and blue and gold
from thin glass globes

we make holidays now
full of light and color
our houses full with juicy smells
our windows like beacons
on december's dark clear nights.

remembering love
whether in fact or wish
we make our holidays
of love

we gather ourselves together out of love
as much as tradition or loneliness.
and if we can find love to spare
we gather as many others
as our hearts will hold.

on our new holy days
we rest enveloped in winter/death
trusting in its promise that spring
will, in its own way,
come.

and we celebrate the holiness
of ourselves and our world
in each other's brightness.
we eat, revering the life
that gives us food.

we breathe outside, together,
on our holidays
to come back to ways we've lost
and the knowing that our holidays
are about stars that were bright
long before and after jesus
at this sacred time each year

when the earth clears off its
ornaments, shows itself bare
for us to see, to listen,
in these holy days,
to its soul

sometimes we do not speak
your eyes ask   give me food
my departing legs answer
you are a hunter
do not abase yourself
begging on country paths.
sometimes we speak
you say   touch me
i ask
curl on my lap and smile.
sometimes we see each other
and call out greetings.

<u>valentine</u>   (for e. b.)

i have wanted so much from life
now here i sit this valentine's eve
counting in smaller numbers
smiling at sloganed sugar hearts
my sister's phone call on company time.
and it's raining, i must include that
must pack away
in the fluted cups of my heart-shaped box
solitude with faint guitar
lemony carrots that turned out right
the slow softness of this night
and that, after yesterday full of hard words,
you and i can still forgive.

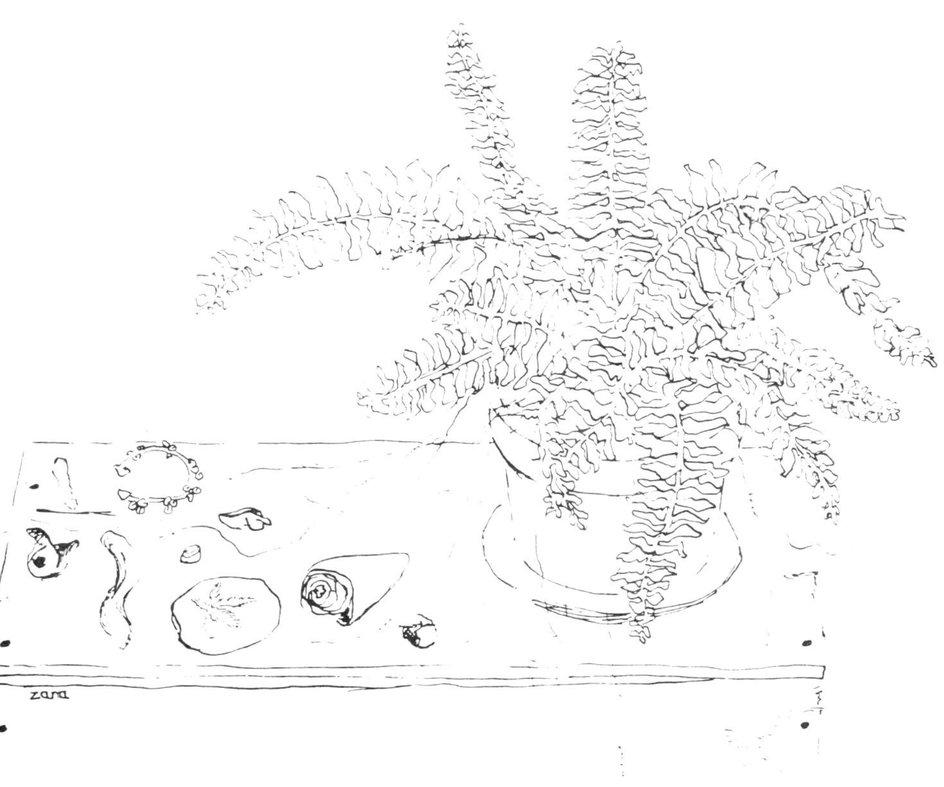

<u>rena's grandma died</u>

and tonight she's back from new york
just in time for sunday dinner
and those of us who drink liquor
have amaretto in her grandma's crystal glasses
admiring the purple rug that rena
says we can use in the living room
and the toaster oven she brought back
and the china cats.
we balance plates on laps
arl who can't find a way to make money
lucia who has an infection in her tubes
loraine whose son has just left for the winter
marj and gani and sharon, fugitives
from a bad scene at another farm.
we eat our garden's yellow squash, fried,
with home-canned ketchup made by jay.
arwen twirls in her little dress, hands me
green ribbons to roll into ringlets for her hair.
dishes done, we collect land payment cash
volunteers to pick peaches tuesday
and who will turn off the rain-bird.
we scatter to long-distance phone calls
pee breaks, bedtimes for those
rising early in the morning.
rena straightens the wool blanket on the couch.
it looks good with the new rug.
i'm tired, forget to hug her on my way
out the back door to my cabin.
but sara's still there, and marj
smoking on the back porch--
maybe rena will join them for a cigarette
before goodnight.

blood dark in moonlight
my stain upon the sheet
i no longer own sheets
with semen stains   nor even
marked with another womon's blood

here with sisters
my thoughts
rarely   incestuous
threatened by the fragility
of our careful web

yet this night, with waxing moon
i lie waiting, on old blood stains
longing for flesh soldered against flesh
waiting as if
for someone

<u>porcupine</u>

your eyes, searching the dark window
for mine, if i could stay to watch
you and baby, snug together
selecting blackberry leaves...
but we have waited months to catch you
i must call others to come with garbage cans
and rip you from this quiet night.
your nose sparkles, your face
trusts a kind world, but
alert for something else.
sudden cans and lights--you plunge
not too fast for us
but too among the brush and
beneath my cabin.
marj corners your baby
refuged in sympathetic brambles.
but in the morning the upended can
that we would take to king mountain
stands empty, weight still in place
baby burrowed out the bottom
through a mat of weed.
and loraine says, well i guess
it was her again gnawing on the barn
last night,
and we all smile.

<u>the things that change</u>

i sit in the grass filling my hat with mushrooms
like last spring and the spring before
in this spot, and with the same hat...
this is for the things that do not change.

rain fell meager in this spring of '82
and the mushrooms, small and shriveled,
huddle in nests of dead grasses.
last year i filled my hat full
and had some left for drying.
this is for the things that change.

in that year since the big mushrooms
an orange cat has died
a womon and two children left the land
two children and six wimin came.

i avoid the eyes and path of someone
whose sight i loved then.
someone i hated has gone and returned;
we feel out ways to know each other's lives.

i wanted rules about numbers of dogs
and who could make noise where, when.
now those things drift over in their own flow
like clouds shifting, warmth to sorrow.
things move, and move again.

my legs are worse this year.
i no longer hunt mushrooms up near woods edge
but only these a few steps from my cabin.
it is impossible to know if i will ever be well
if my friend and i will ever laugh and sing again
if the water table will hold enough
for all the wimin on this land.

but this year salsify puffs dot the field
where there were none before
and afternoon thunder tempers our flat, hot days
so i know that it is possible to hope.

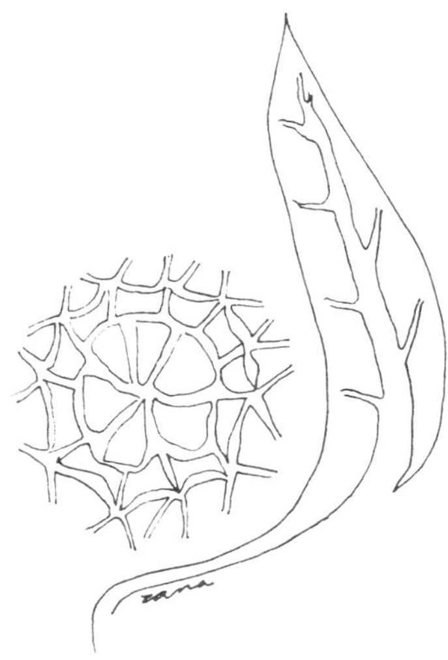

sea maid

<u>wrap me in violets</u>

they come back to me
as premonitions: sea maid
walking on daggers
princess bruised by pea

wrap me in violets
wrap me in silks
float me on cloudfur
to my home

my body sends up its
white flags
over and over
but in vain:
no one waits
for my surrender

body once so firm
climbing hard hills, running
the bases fearlessly
now must fear
falls, even jars
even sleeping
in the wrong position

must live the life
of an old womon
why? at 31

why, on bright days
when i could be walking
miles in my pleasure
why, on dark days
aching alone
in my grey room

wrap me in violets

betrayed
betrayed by once-strong
flesh, betrayed
by earth that taught me
its secret trails
betrayed by whatever
made me love
independence

by doctors who
pistol-whipped me
with their pills
by friends
who can't be bothered
remolding my niche
in their lives

wrap me in silks

they come back to me
as premonitions:
elizabeth on her dreary couch
carson drinking sherry-tea

daggers

sometimes i laugh
we joke about my
carved-wood cane
they gathered
like doves around
my hospital bed

and i have had time
for once, blessed
time, days
itinerants
without customshouses
to answer to

but o, i have hardly
touched this earth
as i was meant to do.
have i exhausted so many
of this world's promises
in three decades?

float me on cloudfur
float me on violets
let me go home

<u>telling</u>

you
you say
you need my voice
to tell what it is like
from day to day   the pain
how it eats into my life
and what my activities are
from dawn to bedtime.
describe a typical day
so we can know.
how long your exercises take
and what you do with
your time.

what is
the typical day
of an easter islander?
maybe you should
send in an anthropologist
to observe my ways
i am too involved
to see the picture whole

and talking about it
or writing about it
is like handling hot coals
so i'm writing about writing about it
instead

sunlight chokes this small room
i continue making lines
head pulsing   joints screaming
my hot sweat
the black odors of india ink
and promised lightning

hard, threatening music
leans against my pen
i feel sharp points insisting
in my flesh and i wonder
if this is only body pain   where
the boundary
is

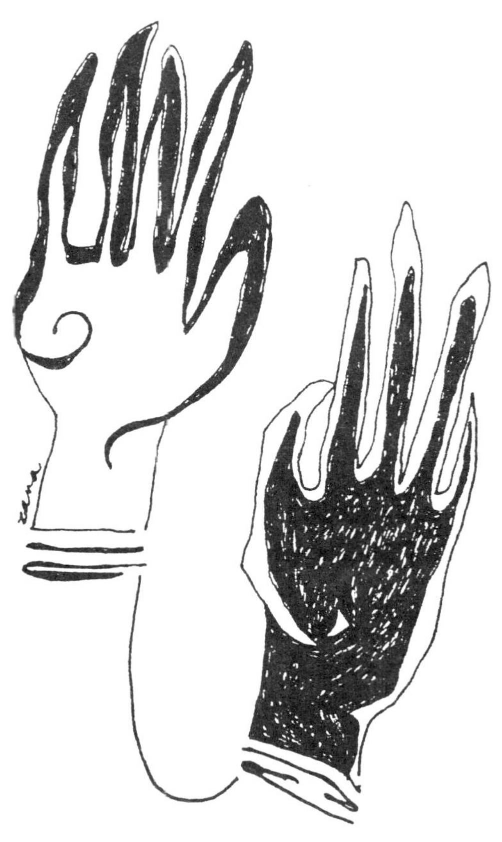

<u>potato sprouts</u>

for soup i scrub these
old potatoes, sprouting
because i haven't had
strength to scrub
i still don't but
there is nothing else to eat
and they will soon go bad

looking up from the sink
outside, seven sisters
pour the concrete privy hole
work hard
i work hard to scrub potatoes
the pain in my arm like fire

i will praise their hard work
no one praises me for scrubbing
and cutting up potatoes

their pinking eyes
poke out at me
like suicide

mocking my life here
and the lonely land
that lies between us
beyond this pane of glass

passing, on a trip to town

i walk in, you see me.
you do not see me.
seconds ticking in my head
you take your time, you chat.
if i explained, it would take longer.
to find a chair, to ask
if accident or disease, and
have it tried this doctor, that vitamin.
i am dis-eased by your world.
it was never built for me.
i used to use a cane
mostly to announce my situation.
it was one more thing to carry
didn't help my leg but hurt my hand
and everyone assumed i had what i needed
my cane, so kept their seats on buses
just the same.
so i pass
for "real," for "whole"
not like those pitiful souls in wheelchairs
whose condition you cannot ignore
though they too are assumed
to have what they need:
chairs, parking places and ramps--
what more could they want?
i want you to hear
that my whole day's energy
is spent buying thread and groceries.
i want you to hear
that i am not the only one.
we pass, not even knowing
who all we are
clenching teeth against the pain
wishing
for a day of ease
in this constant war

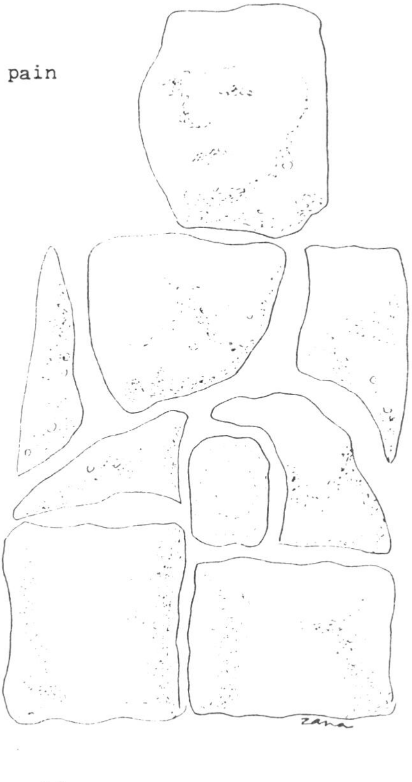

falling
in the mud in the grass among wood chips
near the woodshed near the sawhorse
in the dark
saying no as i have always
caught myself
going down
proud of still sure feet
saying no
but this time
continuing anyway
this time
falling
hard
on the way down feeling
turning over in bed
losing it
falling
far, deep
with no grip on anything
nightdream terror
off the bed
off the world
off reason
and suddenly lying
here
chin in the dirt
banging my brains against stars
a sprawled killed chicken
in the mud in the wood chips
light flashing on the near grass
wet from rain
in the dark in the wet of
no! i can catch myself
surefooted even as
joints erode and muscles atrophy
in that wet terror
sobs tear
into screams

<u>i walk to the garden today</u>

after a month in bed.
it is half as far as i can usually walk:
down from my cabin to the mailbox.
i choose late
for my adventure
breeze cooling my skin like water
pushing away the day's lazy heat.
slowly, carefully, past the privy
past rena's window, reaching for a blackberry.
sara is outside stripping mint from stalks
she warns the garden's been neglected.

but o what wonder to swing open that old gate
under the fat moon rising pale in blue sky
to sit on straw and pull carrots from dark earth
where the stones hold in day-warmth
mallow roots deep and i almost start weeding
automatic, my perpetual chore
but this is a holiday   i celebrate
sitting under the moon as sun levels
through the big madrone, its last light
my joy is described by tomatoes
waiting hidden in their leaves
round and large and red with juice
i gather them lovingly
after two years without
i can eat them again
what is it like to live unrestricted
memory fails me, amazed by the thought

<u>pioneer</u>

i don't know how to do this.

today at grace's house rare winter sun
lit the grass no more than twenty feet
outside the shield of glass.
someone is reading poetry but all i hear
is the shouting of that green sunshine

i don't know how to ask this
that someone pull and tug my wheelchair
over and up and down and out
into that sweet suburban yard.

i save my asking for the big things:
wood chopping, meals when i'm too sick,
getting me here today at all.

claire says, "you're a pioneer!"
who tries to live in the country
where the standard is tough country dyke
and wheels must struggle over rock, through mud

ironically, it's concrete and leaded air
that helped tear me down--
now the cities pay with curb cuts,
disabled parking zones.

i don't know
how to do this
no one is showing me

can my "living in the country"
be reduced to lust for fifteen minutes
of suburban sun?

at home, the cedars crush against blue sky
so far above my bed.
i love to watch
the six rectangles of light and evergreens
how they change
as the day's hours pace by
predictably.

i know that i would rather
see wildness and rarely touch it
than not see <u>or</u> touch.
the sun so out of reach
the stream that i can only hear
soothe by their presence--
though sometimes they pull at me deeply,
under my flesh.

i do not know
how to stop this wanting.

i remember the feel of the climb
feet finding stoneholds under leaf
arms sure, grasping at branches
in the wisp-edge of danger

this is another climb
out of the sharp noon-light
to the shaded soft tops of trees
to a healing place where rain
touches inside my flesh
washes at the angers

leaves me eyes-open for a new plan.

grove

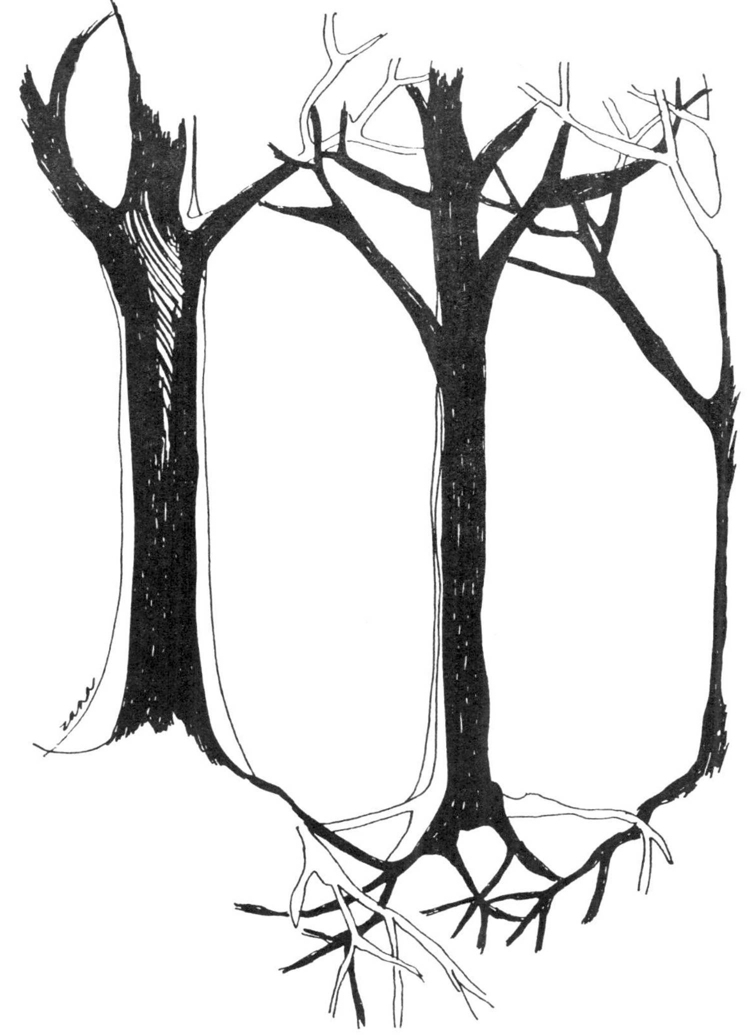

<u>quilt</u>

i used to see the rolls of colored fabric
nestled neatly in grandma's sideboard
    when i started my quilt she sent muslin bags
    filled with a kaleidoscope of scraps
        now i pull her life up around me
        on gray cloud mornings

blue rosebuds, these gathered for a dress she wore
with little blue buttons and dainty lace
"i have to wear tiny prints," grandma said
"because i'm a tiny woman. not like you, dear."
she flipped their mattresses every day of her married life
with those arms, like a wrestler's.
grandpa towered more than a foot above her, cowered
when their wills clashed

twin designs--yellow posies and pink--
hundreds of flowers crushed with their green leaves
onto the small squares of cloth.
the aprons she made from them
mom and i stored in drawers
they were what she knew how to give

tight-checked ochre gingham
color of walls in the house where they lived
through the depression, the war, space missiles,
births of their grandchildren
the house stayed and they stayed with it
right outside of new york city while new york changed
and their only daughter moved a thousand miles southwest

speckled blue pears, dancing in rows
as perfect as the smooth white syrupy canned ones
she opened for dessert
completely unlike
the thick-skinned bird-pecked seedy juicy grapes
grandpa grew in the back yard and offered us proudly

their love was like the bright pink hearts
that appear again and again
outlined in pink pin pricks
regimented in straight lines
he said he adored her and proved it
living without dog or motorcycle
just quietly
hoarding rare trips with a pal to montreal

under the grape arbor in summer
with fine stitches she hemmed prints like this
scattered handful of wildflowers
some sad twilight blue
others the scarlet so sudden so often
among my quilt's pastels
as vivid as her garnet birthstone ring
as startling as her first blood

she ran to her brother, terrified
showing her body's voiceless wound
her mother slapped her for that
without explanation
abby was a bad girl
who kept change from grocery money
to buy herself pickles
she was not her mother's favorite, nor her father's
she was a bad girl who at twenty-four
gave birth to a child put in her womb by a sailor
long since returned to sea
she had understood no more why the blood stopped
than what started it in the first place

was she wearing tiny dots and cabbage roses by the time
her pretty sister's boyfriend fell in love with her
offering marriage and a name for the child?
the family had moved by then, in shame.
hidden in the attic for two years
the baby wobbled on rickets-ravaged legs
     only after joe's proposal did abby admit
     motherhood of the sickly girl

mom has always liked green
not shy spring yellow-greens
but the strong evidence of a full season's growing.
here's a pattern grandma chose for her:
muted blue-green acorns, rusty leaves
peace, stillness--mom's lifelong striving
after the years of hard words, broken dishes, tears

so grandma gave her this: green aprons.
she knew exactly the right designs and colors
after all, my mother was her only child
mom was the one who used to get the rags
to wipe blood from the kitchen floor
where grandma stood doing dishes
mom dragged her to a doctor at age fifty
came to see her in the hospital
where they cut out the tumor and vaginal obstruction
that had made sex painful for thirty years

that was before we moved away
that was when grandma and daddy still raged weekly
later she had to tell mom how to live her life by mail
the snake under her sweet smile
twisted through her careful script
we opened her letters anticipating venom

but i looked forward to packages from grandma
the sweaters bought on sale
the remnants of mom's childhood that mom wouldn't have saved
the bright strips of grandma's cloth

grafting her patterns onto my life
building my quilt slowly
off and on over ten years
with no quilting frame
nor preordained design
at random, seams uneven
a piece of work so unlike
her tidy stitchery
she wouldn't have quite hidden
her disdain

gradually, patterns finding their own form
juxtaposing my own crying out and hers
making us sisters in pain

making me dream, lying under soft quilt
with mom and grandma, flying

patiently
making
small stitches
joining the edges of our lives
for strength that works
both ways

<u>moonstone</u>   (for carol)

i loved the ring you wore,
a misty light-circled moonstone
on a silver band. your hands
were like mine used to be,
dimpled and soft like plump bread dough.

the day that jimmy
tore my loving with doped-up words
your hand with the ring reached
into the back seat to comfort me
and i held it tight against my cold face.

you were sleeping when i finally got there
after your child died.
like a little dead bird your hand
rested on the white sheet
and it was such a young, soft hand
wearing nothing but that simple ring.

<u>grandpa, at 82</u>

82 this year and you've cut me off
beyond my power to say or do
i bang my fists and swear
i end up face to face with the packet
tied in white ribbon
postcard of a dog on top
remember you wrote
this is terrible the terriblest terrier
remember
rolls of film you sent, urging pictures
and the questions--
my letters were lists of answers
yes daddy's car is a v8
we are all over the flu
our dog is no particular kind
carol is in the first grade now.
remember
you wanted to know
more than i could say
why not get parts in plays
win beauty contests
have a boyfriend
drive a car
be wonderful, be everything
grandpa
where did you get such ideas?
remember
sandwiched between weather details
the doom--cuba, mr. khruschev
move back up north before mexico goes commie
and i said, yes
build bomb shelters
vote goldwater
control
it all
you said, muggings at the world's fair
wops moving into the neighborhood
race riots
then i said
eugene mccarthy, end war in vietnam
still, <u>we</u> said
mint marks on nickels
yellow tomatoes this year
peonies
remember

but the break came as it was sure to
not of your making of course
grandma always grandma
blacklisting various relatives
in different years.
your loyalty is a lead weight, grandpa
that first break you couldn't take it
remember you sneaked a christmas card
from her stack, addressed it to me
with only your name signed.
it meant more to me than any present
but
this second time now
we are both completely adults
she has done it again
though it is you who mouth the words.
remember
i am completely an adult
old enough to discern string trails
in this tangled mat of yarn.
mom says
her again,
grandpa the sacrificial lamb
nervous collapse from worrying
reach out to a man near death
and i say with great sorrow
my grandfather is near to death
my grandfather is a collaborator
i bang my fist
i can no longer live their game
no matter what the time
but i am not so sure
that's my final word

<u>duncanville, 1973</u>

so here you are, mom
down in the "bottom"
elaine and i walk past dead car bodies
down the parched pale dirt road
cracking in july heat

the paths on your dry skin
o mom, just like <u>them</u>
the texans in our lives
all those years

i loved the house in baltimore
but i was nine years old
daddy chose the flat summer lawns
outside of dallas
still too bulldozer-dead
to nurture any life but grass spiders
their speechless hollowness plaguing my days

what did you choose
mom, standing there
crying in the driveway
at our new house?

i marked off the years
i left, san francisco-bound
jim said i'd be back
i said, ridiculous

planning to take you away
nothing holding you now
daddy 14 miles away still in the tract house
but no

elaine and i scuff the dust
talk beneath feather shadows of mesquite
she sounds like <u>them</u>, this sister
without memory of baltimore lushness
without memory of anything but this.

30

mom, even you now say "pe-con"
socialize not with poets but
ruby with her gap-toothed smile,
mama nancy.
sun slaps your thin blue trailer walls
under old trees.

maybe it chose you finally
or the plant cast out helpless
nudged a hopeful root through inhospitable soil.

all this in one desert afternoon:
i've seen you real,
shaken my idea
of home.

weeds and water

white chimney smoke

rising,

joins

morning fog

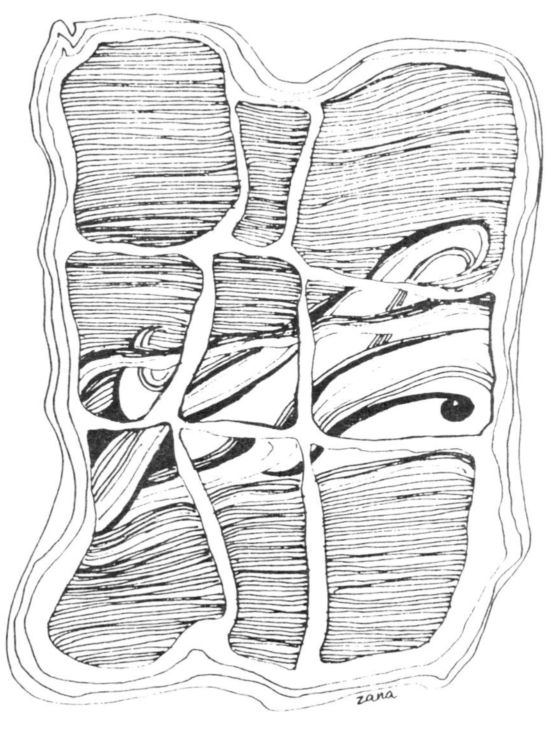

<u>toward home</u>

in darkness
my bed floats
swept by songs
of the wind and rain.
in these hours
who hurries light
with its illusions?
this night's truth:
the warm cave in the forest
has always been there
really
and without light-blinding,
my fingers
know the way.

i will eat meat
for do i not kill
just as truly that
which holds green blood?
i will eat meat
and i will cut
the squash from its vine
and i will touch
their bloods
reverently
knowing i must give much
because i so take

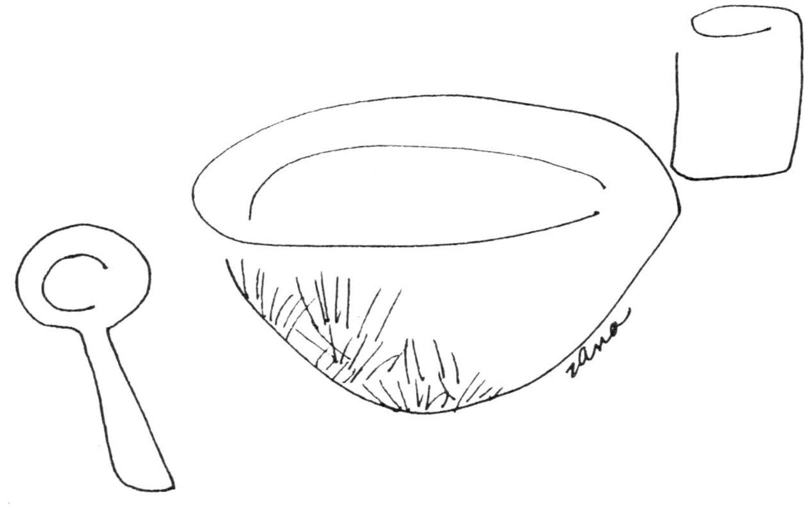

<u>embrace</u>

two days now
you clasp its shiny blue body
in feathery arms
so still you yourself
appear dead.
the quiet web
hammocks other bodies
perfect, intact
like russian easter eggs
your handiwork
the sucked-out shell.

<u>concrete</u>

at the edge of the runway
there are small purple flowers
there are grasses making seeds
there is a stand of rushes
around a low spot where
water settles
directed there by culvert
directed to where
it can be
out of the way

the weeds are
out of the way
they won't give
plane passengers
hay fever

you can't stop
weeds and water
you can only push them
out of the way

sometimes even that is hard
water seeps into concrete basements
till it floods them
weeds grow from every small crack in the city
sometimes, i have heard,
a mushroom spore
gathering force in the soil
has pushed determinedly through
to shatter a sidewalk
with the soft weightlessness of its head

runways are not a flimsy crust
like sidewalks.
they are built like highways
with complete seriousness.
nothing breaks through.

but there's a certain kind of eyes
that look at runways and see

the layers beneath,
the clay that once took shape in daily pots
the different-hued layers of rock and stone
each remembering millennia

and the loam
harboring weed seeds--
weed seeds can lie dormant
underground
for a very long time.

car trip

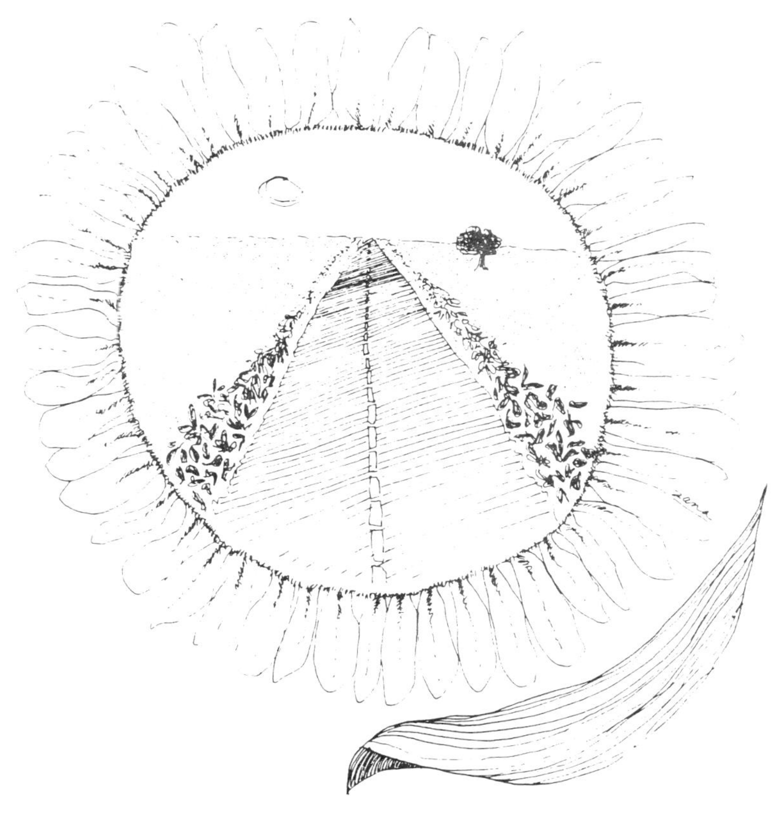

your face is softest in repose
wide grins do not become it.
i used to know that but forgot
and carry your smiles around
inside me for hours now.

<u>car trip</u>

a car trip is part of falling in love
a car trip with people who don't know
jabbering about plutonium and poetry
up there in the front seat; the back seat
is quiet and filled with the flowers
i gather for you from every garden and meridian
the armloads of treetops and cabbages i catch for you
the clean gray of concrete and the sky
and my solitude.

i lay in bed last night trembling awake with my heartbeats
and still my body races faster than the car
skimming through grass fields, smiling at the sky.
i want to pull this ceaselessness inside me
then let you take it, shining, from my eyes.

<u>beginning a goodbye</u>

i remove your collar
phone number written inside
in case some nice person
finds and keeps you

your fur blows into my lungs
my lights burn at 3 a.m.
sitting up, smoking coltsfoot
pouring cups of yerba santa tea

for eleven dollars a week they'd inject
cat essence into my flesh, but
i don't have eleven dollars a week
even for you

they told me exposure
would make it worse
but you were already here then
purring me to sleep at night

your little mother-seeking body
curled inside the crescent
my body made; waiting
your turn when lovers spent the night

who will take you,
no longer new-kitten?
we wait, you sleeping in the bathroom
me breathing my vaporized air

i remove your collar
and for the first time
you're free of my possession
we are equals now

you can leave if you please
no one will call me
no one will pack you in a box
and bring you back

go hunting, ananka,
these long summer days
find someone to adopt you
thinking you have no other home

don't make me be the one
to plot you out of my life
let me come home one evening
and find you gone

<u>by the gate</u>

my love for you
unfolded slow, was like
a girl becoming womon
in an old frame house
she somewhat liked,
that felt like home
although she cursed her drafty room
and thought white clapboard so, so plain

there were secrets she had learned:
oyster-mortar cellar walls
blackened wood beneath a rug
and the funny squeak of
that stairstep near the top

one evening coming home
she and friend stood by the gate
and as they talked her eyes
dilated all around the clapboard frame,
her heart awoke.

<u>cycle</u>

your letters rip apart
the smooth paper of my days

i dream of you sometimes
the night before one comes

i read each over and over
smothered by your presence

afterwards sweet and sour
swirl in my aching mouth

for days i push back my own
words straining at fingertips,

beating in brain until fragments
burst into showers of pages of script

i see it off safely, then wait a month
or more to glimpse your heart again

<u>japanese robe</u>

in my japanese robe i dreamed of you
before you knew i was dreaming
sang songs, drew poppies
while you were lost in your dream of her
i didn't know
we are both so good at secrecy
and in the night when i waken
the dark flooded with
your lonely porch light
you are at her house arguing
trying to spend the night while she says
can't you be happy for just what is?
in her japanese robe, in one smooth turn
she shuts her door.

you say toward me you feel sisterly.
now i bundle in a woolen robe.

she asks me to breakfast.
i don't care if i go.

she holds the sash.
is she closing the circle now?

half the time
i outline you blankly
not knowing what i'd do with your body
if i had the chance.
mine is not a simple desire
it creeps up and flashes on me suddenly
weeding the peas while you plant
or over the wildflowers on sunday dinner's table.
then i want you too much to touch you
and, the same as with the sun,
i can only snatch glances and then away.
anyone but a fool would take off across the continent.
instead i tend my fortress
leaning back up against that door
you've walked out of too many times.
i dream your regrets and return
i glimpse my own clear strong love
briefly from the corner of an eye.
but mostly there's desire and hate and tenderness
blinding me with migraine
as we sip our tea
divvy up the phone bill
sit in circle with sisters.
someone tell me one more choice
beyond the fortress, the accident victim,
the get-away.

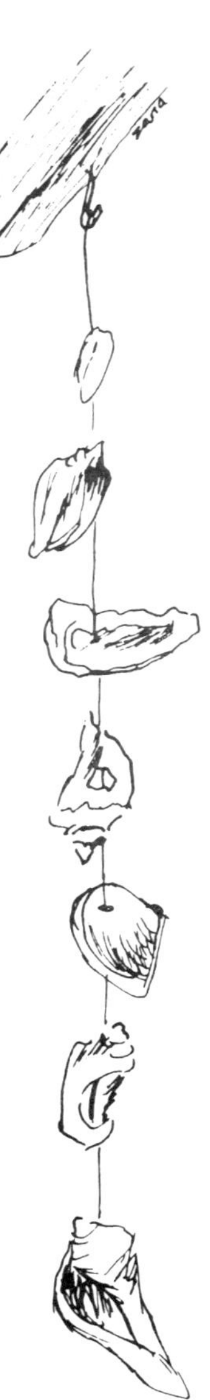

love poem

there is not much left for you.
all those men i died for, yes
i really tried to love and care
even the kindest of them threw me
took his turn and flung me
on cement   my bones cracking
the marrow leaking into soil.

i grin but i have been a tender soul.
i'm bitter, but i've loved like the sun.
too much, more than any one of them
could understand.
my bones broke
from the strain.
i hurt all day now and doubt
anyone will want to love me
in that way.

you do.
but dear, there's so little left for you.
to come and see me in my bed
or sit out on my porch awhile.
i cannot even release my heart
into your care.

and yet you come.
listening, constant.
i rage against you
to scare you away if you be false.
you come.
i hear your story:
what has torn me down
layered the thickness of your walls.
will we ever understand?

i lie in grass
alone.
alone with the pain
it is easier not to share.
give me time to think.
can your love be real?
i must reeducate my life:
give me time.

<u>i've loved you across fields</u>

i've loved you across fields and through fog
on the wild plains and from mountaintops
all the way to the top of the sky
and down inside my toes moving in the dawn.
i love you tangled in vines, moss-soft,
rainbow-gleaming on cat's fur
and in other people's eyes.

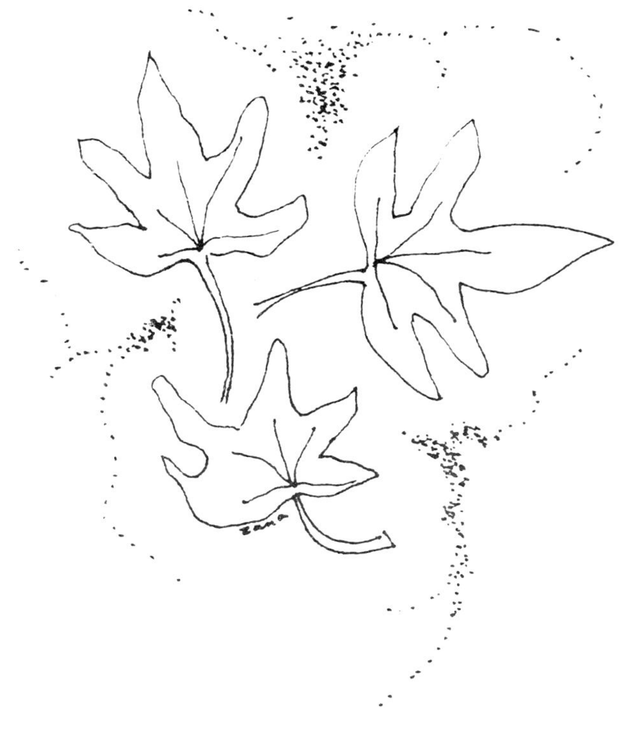

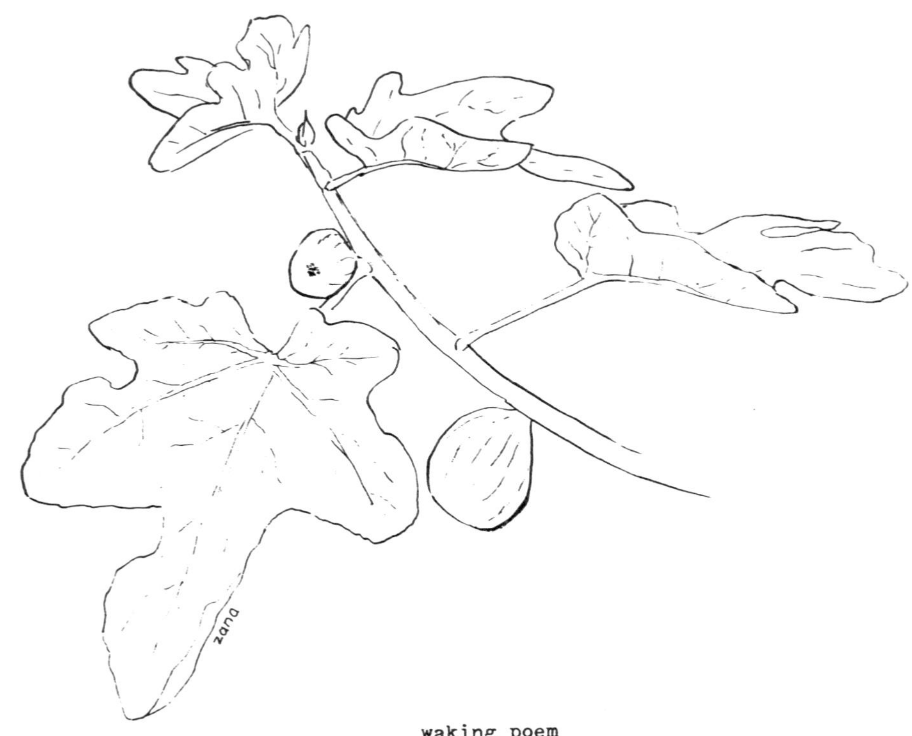

waking poem

now we come to the end of the map
can i reach around my anger
can you reach behind your fears
and trembling in the cold
guided only by stars
together trace new pathways
not on paper
but through our lives?

an unclaimed hour

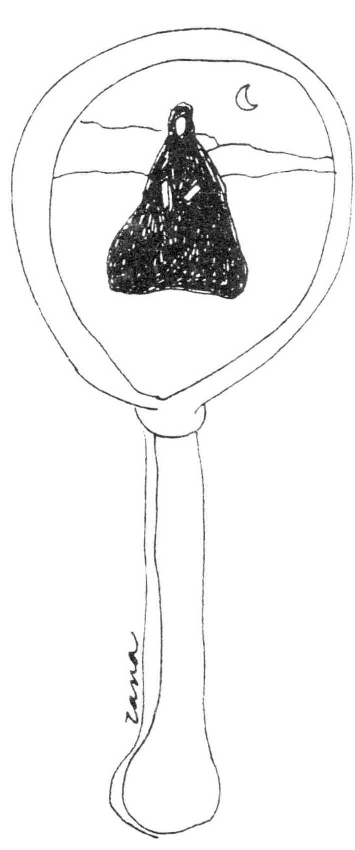

harvest time: i gather in nostalgia
and you, sherri, after all this time.
going back, the layers of years
the husbands, the houses
the states, the jobs
illness, manic depression--
both of us, in our separate ways.
your daughter, thirteen this year
and i have never met her.
you called me once on a WATS line
from chicago to arkansas--o sherri
your voice was just the same
the past was yesterday

you write of talents wasted, solitude
you doubt you'll ever know.
i've acted on my talents, had such solitude
it's nearly swallowed up my life.
and you in your marriage, that stability
i have envied, too.
in dreams we have a meeting place, perhaps.

even in life there is a crossing:
you outgrow fulltime motherhood
i live along with other wimin's kids.
your loneliness strikes a different tune than mine
a steady lover but rare friends
while i sing with many friends but no true lover
in all these years.

all these years.
seventeen.
and that's the age we were
the year we met.
go back
tonight
by candle
as autumn
changes the seasons

<u>for w. t.</u>

there is nothing between us.
there is not the barrier of polished wood-width.
no white starched garment declaring its rank.
you don't pat me with cardboard hand.

your hands are cool but i feel their warmth.
our eyes touch and you would recognize me, clothed,
in another part of town.
you have taken blood from my vein with your own hands.
my story is part of your own.
there is much between us.

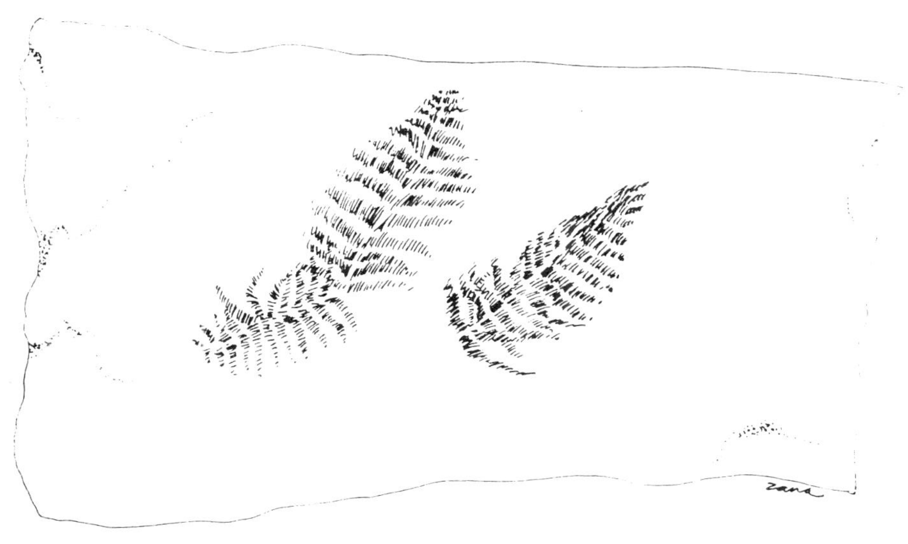

<u>anarcha</u>

who were you
body split apart
thirty times
fogged only by
slow-death opium
slave womon
your cries echo
in my veins

the surgeon learned
knife routes on you
j. marion sims,
"father of gynecology"
past president of the AMA
imaged in metal at three schools

and you, anarcha
one of seven
he cut
six nameless others
live for us in you

o anarcha
such endless pain

<u>preacher's wife</u>

on her knees
among green berries
fat, strong, discolored hands
laying reeds of straw.
straws of white hair poke
from under wide brim.
each day she works
the sun hours.

gardener's husband
writes words about god
inside, under bulb light.

55

december, holly
your smooth ageless face
snuggled in strands of colored wool
your body layered in
soft skirts and pants and jackets
cocoon and butterfly all at once
such cradled grace
and in the old red truck
everything about everyone
but you spoke it slow
always slow, womon of earth
i knew you were, then
wise as silent olmecs
smoothed in stone, south
where their hot bloods
mixed with clay
you, fire and earth womon
i knew even then
before spring brought your hair
gold and playing from winter cap
before clover-sweet summer
sang your body out along the air
smooth and strong and quiet as madrone limb
no accident we meet over herbs
flesh warms flesh easily
music weaves our lives strong
you renew my earth ties
and for you, holly
this song

<u>on my father's side</u>

after we laughed and kissed
enjoyed our food and wine
talked films and politics

then came the quiet
moon hidden by trees and shadows
outlining the creases in your face
the kinship horror creeping
from its secret places

tattoos
ledgers of experiments
you said perhaps it should no longer
be mentioned, but then
you said, no...

<u>desert landscape</u>

      1.

be in my movie.
i need some freeze frames
some slow motion scenes
you are too close and fast
a lightning lizard
under my gaze

      2.

i catch glimpses
of the veins in your arms.
another human body
so foreign it terrifies me
how can your arms be so thin
why do the words come from your mouth
in ways i barely understand?
and yet our eyes are a similar color
as they ooze into each other like river mud.

      3.

the fear?
  betrayal.
that you would betray i have no doubt:
        you are a man.
i think that you are not a cruel man
nor a lax one but   a man you are
and so betray me simply
by not knowing who i am
and i do not choose to spend my life
      telling you.

      4.

how is it that i can use
the word love
to think of you?
    i can only find what i love
    by eliminating things:
    your looks, interests,
    how you talk about wimin,
    what you do with your life

...but there is a certain kindness

5.

stranger
walk into a desert night
with me
let darkness slow us
into brief, sweet wordlessness
overwhelming everything
with the fact of our touch

6.

witches
loved among their own kind
but on festival nights
rolled with their opposites
on the hot dark ground
i don't know how to do that
today
when your race
holds mine captive.
still, it's my weakness
to always glimpse human flesh
here and there beneath
the khaki of police

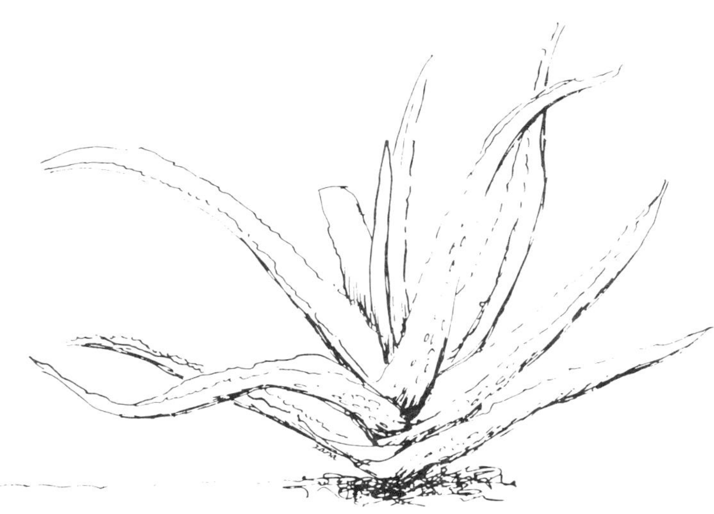

<u>heathcliff</u>

i wake from long sleep, grieving,
the taste of blood blurred in my mouth
blurred with the not knowing who
for moments, not remembering whose
are these helpless hands, pale under tan skin.

outside my window, leaves sing joyously green
inches beyond my reach. all i touch
is heavy old wood, waterlogged with tears.
yes, the brief interlude is over.

now once again you feel to me
soft and cool and evanescent as fog. but cathy
i <u>saw</u> <u>your</u> <u>face</u> last night--
in the deep tunnel to which only you have the key
my hands gripped your arms and felt
bloodwarmed flesh!

listening to a survivor

there are small
very fine
lines
on her cheek
a soft cheek
still imaginable as
that young
when he
broke into her body

thieves
at least
do not call it
love

she has seemed
sinewy
to me
compact and
held in
but

a wisp of
tender hair
grazes that soft
cheek
and she
is ten
again

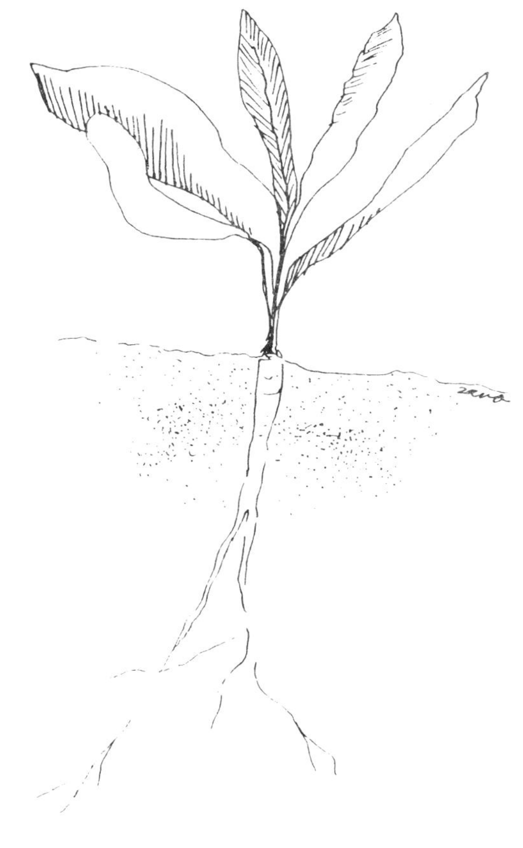

we don't know when something's ended
we don't know because to know
would be to know the future
see through all the mirrors
back all the way to death.

so someday there may again
be an unclaimed hour
when our appointment suddenly
appears on that mercurial
calendar

eucalyptus
zana

how the wind hurts

when you're stripped bare

like a peach cut open

slashed by cold steel-blade of air

and you who come so close

from you i turn my eyes

because it hurts too much

to open cleanly, without lies

  (from hans christian andersen)

her face had become like a pink rose--
she willed it to; no more a sea anemone.
she smiled a pink rose smile and he saw
her come toward him daintily, gingerly,
and--he thought--too shy to speak.

inside her the sea
crashed against vein walls,
daggers stabbed at the rosy new legs
once powerful, painless and silvered with armor.
her short stub of tongue still tasted salt blood.

and still, and still, it was not enough.
he called her his dear devoted child.
on his wedding day she silently
stood watching as he kissed his bride.

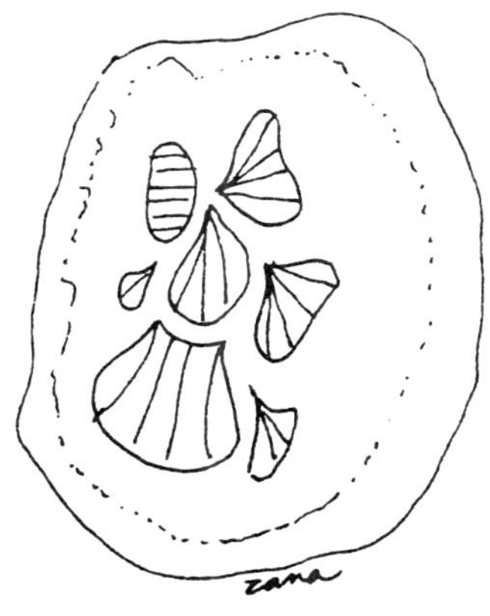

<u>a once-loved face</u>

when we ride together and you drive
your body is too close   your face accessible
i remember myself a year ago
and you.

you required that i stop wanting you
and i complied. into the bargain
i love you less; the two mesh
more than you ever understand.

now it is not so hard not to want you
i can return to beginnings
how i saw you first
little wise old secret lady
fingers full of quilts and cigarettes.

i can see why sex distresses you
after 13 bare years, hugging cats
not letting people pry you open
i thought to go gentler
tempered by the route i'd taken
into loving you
slow knowing deepening respect
saturating my days with soft joy.

but in the end your silence unwound me
my pale blouse blowing out in september wind
my black boots stormed your hill.
and i will always remember
your flat brown eyes.
for a change you sat, i paced
gulping water like it was whiskey.

six months later we're here:
still on this land together
close enough to see each other's lights at night.
you ask me do i still
feel that way.
no.
you breathe relief.
we are uneasy friends
and it is strange
watching you drive
to trace the pitted surface of your chin
i never kissed.

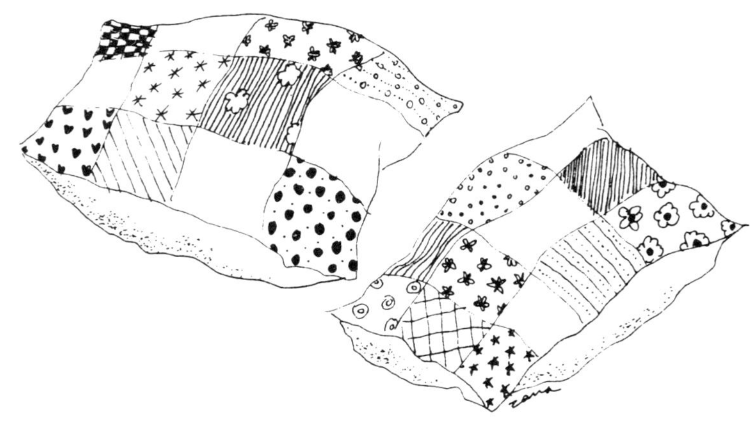

<u>for you, my saint</u>

I.

i keep thinking i should write you:
i'm sorry.
after all
it's <u>your</u> suicidal depression
what right have i to put in all this stuff
about my own needs, to challenge you
to fly out here and face me.

II.

do you remember the madonna
at st. mary's at the foot of central avenue?
we would walk that far, pivot
and walk back to work.
a mile's exercise, wasn't it?
she was so white up there
in her alcove.

III.

some madonna, sleeping around.
but i knew you saw both sides of me.
and you were mine,
chastely married, a friend to outcasts
my big brother and my truest love.

IV.

i am unused to this role with men.
which role? either.
me the madonna, or especially them.
i don't know what to do with your purity.
where the line is between that and fear.

V.

in our ninth year of friendship
so much changes.
once i starved and feasted
at the rich table of your caring
with all its rules and boundaries.
now you write asking for crumbs:
a keep-in-touch letter
to end my long silence.

VI.

my purity is less diluted now.
the frenzy left some time ago
and i am rooted deep in earth.
i live with wimin, love who i live with
like a nun. make love with who i love
like a witch--
they're all the same.

VII.

your terror has starved you out.
you walk lonely, no companion of soul
since i left five years ago
starved of you and mourning and raging.
like mary, the meaning in your marriage
is adoration of the kids.

VIII.

we maintain the faces we have always worn.
but between your neat-typed lines, anguish.
under my fountain of emotions, peace.
my cool white hand tests the fever of your brow.
judges you will live.

IX.

letters are simpler.
they cannot shift, like flesh.
they can be put aside, out of mind.
your love for me can be defined
and not spill over.
my love for you
is wide.

X.

i ask to see you
with some fear, without answers.
how have the fires purified,
how burnt?
we must dig fingers in earth together
holier than madonnas
of smooth white stone.

<u>eucalyptus</u>

i wish that i could
know eucalyptus
its silver-sweet scent
luring bees
upward through leaves
at first round and shining
then lengthening into
evil-eyed sickles

eucalyptus entices me
with cleansing fragrance
promising to heal wounds
but eucalyptus, once i'm here
overpowers me
with the murk of secret rooms
hurls its sickles and piercing
clean sting groundward,
daring me into
its mystery

<u>word failures</u>

                I.

the failures of words word failures the
incomprehensible touching of souls

    across barriers that should be deep
    "hello zana how ya doing today?"
    "hi rube--fine--i'm good--
    beautiful weather we're having."
    "yes, we're lucky."

    arms of water nests of deep
    escape   the pain
    prison of   no words
    i could   touch you
    in a thousand colors
    o rube
    why are we such strangers

    i live in water
    seeing my own hands   blue green
    animals touch and sniff each other out
    without introduction without
    the failures of words
    fish swim close to each other
    in the water all things come equal
    have less weight
    i would swim to you and lie
    quietly by your side, barely touching
    we would absorb each other's lives
    then drift away

                II.

imprisoned
by air
air requires words
to fill it
words like "o rube" and "i love you"
that lock doors not open them
imprisoned in myself
by word failures
my being stretches out to you
on alien air
to say "o rube" and have it mean
and have it mean   ocean
and have it mean   the tender
petals of a flower's opening

                III.

when you say
my name
    you need not say
        any more

                IV.

i want a world where
i can come to you, look into your eyes
and lead you into water-stillness
water-depth.
i want a world where
we are not afraid

                V.

you are as different from me
as a cat, a fish, a wasp.
could i spend hours with you
and wake together in a bed?
i want the joy of spiritbond
that rests in flesh
i want to feel no ends

                VI.

write me a love song like a poem:
sit beside me at dusk
                and say nothing.

                VII.

you are as different from me
as a weed.
shall i pull you up fiercely
from the garden i have plotted
or forgive you and see your beauty?

                VIII.

in the end i will leave here and
not think about you.
thoughts are as transitory
as words.
our different habitats
will overwhelm the fragile thing
that grows between us.
we have both been taught about words,
that they define what is real.
but to myself, in water-depths
of elusive dream
i whisper only the word
love

this week i am several people

i am z, dark and jagged
sideways spying out at you from narrow eyes.
who are you laughing with over there?
why did you dress up tonight?

i am nancy the compassionate nurse
with a silver tray full of remedies
and hugs for your distress
which i even take into my own body
mimicking your symptoms.

i am the lover neither of us has ever had
who would die for you
would suffer through whatever you need
waits patiently
for you to see the light.

i'm the one who understands
takes in that you do not really hate me
that we react to separation in different ways.
i smile down calmly on you
from this place of knowing.

i'm the suicide, the crazy
just barely holding the pieces together
in my square-clenched arms.
i walk around sullen, not speaking
then howl for hours in my cabin.

i am a blind kitten
headed singlemindedly for your warm body
groping, starving,
needing no words no looks nothing
but that.

i am the avenger
of my own lifetime of being wronged
i stand solitary, a sharp stencil in black
my gunmetal aimed at you
across the chasm.

i am the tragic figure
trailing long dark skirts
through the dust of my devastated life.
you set up walls between us to make yourself leave.
i sit outside your walls
weaving intricate patterns in deep colors.

i am the witch of my future self
rippling guitar strings
laying hands and feeling the screams of my body
drawing pictures with children
in the august sun, picking berries
finding how to get through each new hour,
each new day.

witch at evening

in this

new room

where clean light

deflects unhindered

from wall to wall

i hesitate

to intrude

my life's

utensils

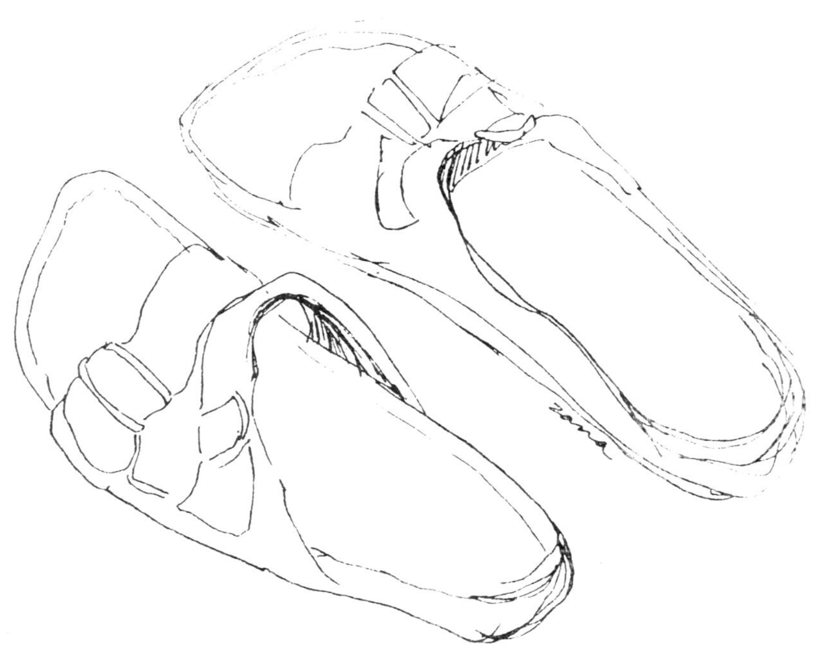

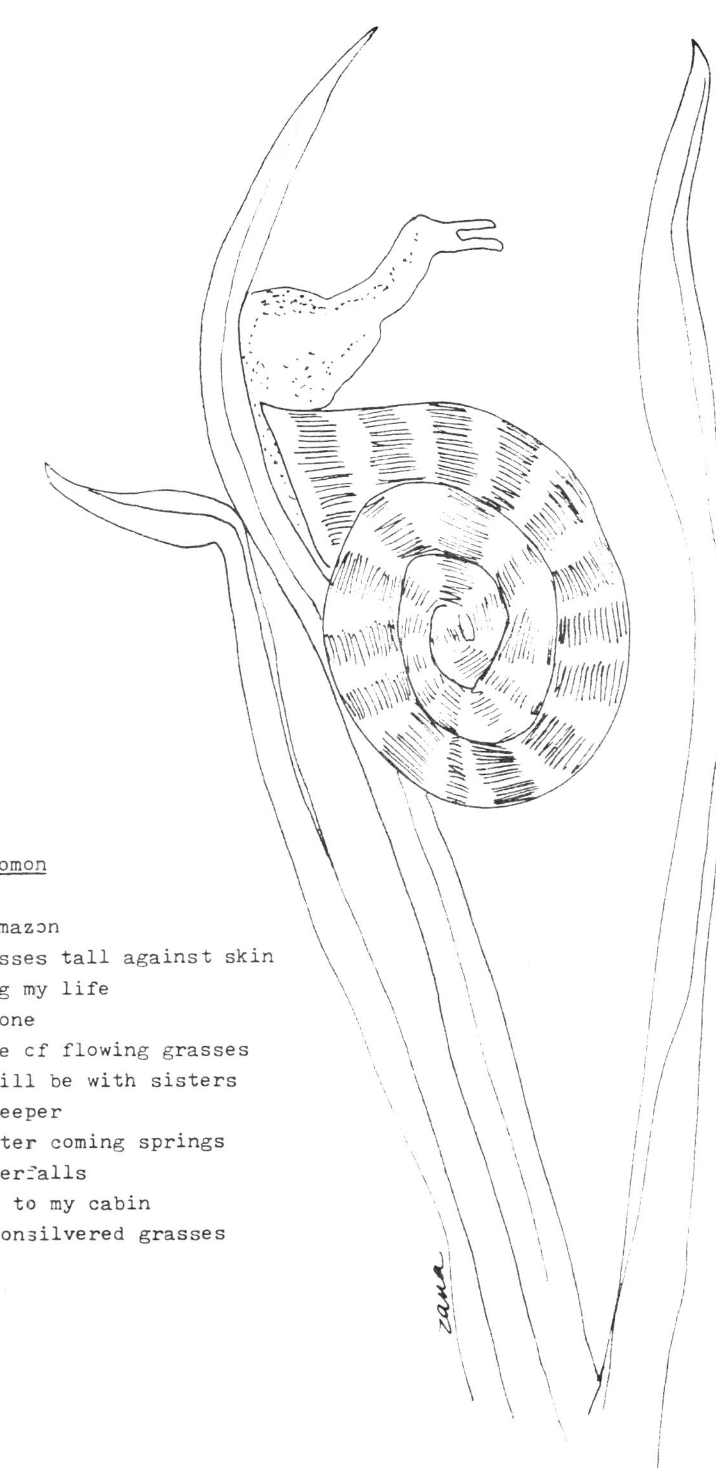

country woman

like an amazon
proud grasses tall against skin
sun baring my life
i walk alone
in silence of flowing grasses
tonight will be with sisters
sharing deeper
dammed water coming springs
maybe waterfalls
then home to my cabin
wading moonsilvered grasses
home

<u>this morning's mirror</u>

well, there is no longer
any vestige of a smile
--is this really my own face?
it's not what i expect
it takes me by surprise
after 33 years

more like the face of a guerilla
not relaxing even in jungle refuge
among ancient mother trees
not even in my own cabin
not even alone with myself
not letting pleasure come in

it is not just a sad face
sadness i would recognize
that has been with me
for all my life
but this, this barricade
that won't be taken down
this fortress against another day
o my soul, when was it built?

somehow i thought
i could learn how to live;
for each ravine crossed
a deeper one comes:
my face in the mirror this morning
is one

<u>after co-counseling</u>

outside the pioneer store
in the car   in the dark
surrounded by cold rain
eating an ice cream sandwich
anonymous
    it is hard to be anonymous
    in a town of 700
    it was hard to be
    anonymous in san francisco
    it is hard to ever
    be anonymous
but necessary
cooling off between worlds
not yet ready for anyone more talkative
than the cigar store indian under the pepsi sign.
    just sitting here quiet in the car
    letting things come clear
    in the rain

i nurture calm
my hands forming around
as if it were an egg
coolly around its whiteness

<u>before solstice, 9980</u>

dark sleep calls me
and i ask
by the blade? by mushroom toxin?
the air is still
the soil does not respond
i lie flattened in orchard weeds
it is almost winter and the sun is not enough
the sun is an inconstant lover   i wonder
will i lie here
till evening
sucks warmth from my marrow?
air moves slightly now
cools where the sun cannot reach
i am not afraid
but i hear
    it is not time
    when it is time you will know
i gather and walk toward home
to build a fire   understanding
the knowing will be my only decision
the how it can happen
will do itself

<u>elusive one</u>

you wake me
at dawn
with a new day
for my delight
you curl around me
and i am a slave
to your essence

and in the quiet
sun day
when i see you
off in the magic hills
you fill me with smiles
or tears
and only we
know why

you
overpower me
your gentle surge
i lie on your shore
waiting gratefully
for your sea to claim me
name me
carry me
where it will

<u>herb womon</u>

slow intimate work
the stripping of thyme leaves
from their stems

it slows me down
their pale green calming my eyes
their soft scent a balm
for the wound of your absence

the skin has its own gratitude
for bare porch boards
warmed by quiet sun

let despair lie
change always comes
do the work
that ties you to earth.

and she said
in your body
i feel a great long loneliness...
you have learned some ways of dealing
with it

she touched my body
here in my room at this spa
i have <u>come</u> here to be alone
to embrace my aloneness
perhaps to come out understanding
it
though these were not reasons
i gave myself

the four pale walls of this room
flatten toward me in innocence
the mirrors, noncommittal
only reflect what is given them
reflect 36 year old me
bare and dark
smooth-faced
innocent

    thirty years ago i stripped an indian doll
    of her sateen and feathers
    wreathed her in a metal bead chain
    and in this she possessed
    the whole forest of our living room
    in ultimate freedom, power and solitude
    she was my only doll whose skin was
    the color of mine
    she was a small cheap plastic doll
    the only one i loved

mirrors can be
hard to look in
there is all the body hair
i remember that time in the park
daddy said   your legs are so shapely
you've got my legs
i loved him for that
for not saying why don't you shave

what think these men here
who flirt with me, or stare
what think the wimin whose legs
have never been allowed
the innocence of hair?

    the indian doll owned one thing:
    two pieces of wood nailed into a couch
    painted silver.
    she was a queen.

i come to this room for a month
with one suitcase
and my silver wheelchair.

at night the walls confine
i am surrounded by the sounds
of other people's televisions
drowning out my silent one
i sit on my single bed
restless for touch
for the fur of the rabbit
who roams here daytimes

    there are so many
    photos of me
    with a cat on my lap

hollow
for human passion
compassion, even
a smile
though the people here
the men are lechers
the wimin think homosexuals
sin against god

i am lonely
i immerse myself
in my loneliness
that never ends
here or at home

i immerse myself

in the water
the shadow of my body
glides along the pool floor
ringed in auras of light

    in grandma's back yard
    i dug moss clumps
    stuck them with flowers
    submerged all in a glass of water
    and this world of beauty
    of silver bubbles
    was my world

by the pool i lie
spending time with harriet the rabbit.
people say, you'll take her home.
i'm a child, they adults
because of how i love.
they pat her and walk by.

    adults on the periphery
    of my world
    said strange things:
    the white-skinned babydoll
    was superior--she cost more
    yet i could find no use for her
    but to crack open her head
    and see how the eyes worked.

in my body
there is a long loneliness.
i watch parts of it disperse
on the air with harriet's fur
with harriet's loneliness;
when my masseuse shakes out her fingers
shakes out her own loneliness

i watch parts of it disperse
when i can touch that in the wimin
which is not homophobia
can touch that in the men
which is not lechery

touch that in myself

    which is familiar
and good
    and comforting

when i have become
my brown-skinned doll
transforming loneliness
to completion

<u>self portrait</u>

witch at evening
stops
watches mist rise
between mountains
follows its patterns
with sounds
as flames arc around wood
in dark iron belly
soup simmers
the last light fades

these poems come together through my moving toward
self-healing and living in lesbian community. i am
36, a pisces, the oldest of four sisters who grew
up in a jewish/WASP family trying to assimilate and
to ascend into the middle class. being disabled with
arthritis and allergies has extended my love of food
foraging into the medicinal realm. i've compiled a
reference of uses of local wild plants, _our land
provides_, and i've recorded a guided meditation
tape, _journey to another life_. i believe that spir-
itual matriarchists can transform the world.